85

Needle Crafts 5

SMOCKING

SEARCH PRESS
London & New York

Smock top. Made of fine wool. The smocking was cabled at the back then freely smocked on the front of the fabric, with added embroidery and beads (Diana Keay).

Introduction

The name 'smocking' is derived from 'smock', an old English word for the shirt-like garments which were usually worn by farm labourers and others engaged in outdoor manual work. This clothing had to allow for ease of movement, as well as afford protection from the weather, so it was usually made from strong material with a certain amount of fullness. To hold this fullness of material in place, a form of decorative gathering evolved which has since become known as smocking.

Today, smocking is used by many of the leading fashion designers on dresses where fullness enhances the style. It can also be used in a restrained way when fashion dictates a less full style. Blouses, skirts, coats, nightwear, hats and bags are all suitable for smocking.

Smocking has always been popular for children's wear, where fullness combined with elasticity for freedom of movement is essential. Infant dresses, christening robes, party dresses both long and short, sun dresses, hats and bonnets are some of the most popular items. And in the home, cushions, pelmets, fixed side-curtains and lampshades are all suitable subjects for smocking techniques.

Because of the many possible textural effects, smocking can be particularly successful when used in creative embroidery pieces. A fabric which reflects the play of light on its ripples and folds like shot silk, or stiff fabrics like taffeta or satin can all be worked on with interesting results.

Method

Fabric for smocking should be approximately three times the width of the finished size needed. Before the decorative stitches can be applied, it should be prepared on the wrong side with transferred lines of evenly-spaced dots. Still working on the wrong side, these dots are picked up with tacking stitches worked in lines, gathered up and tied in place. The fabric is then turned over on to the right side where it is ready for the decorative smocking stitches which will hold the gathers in position. These can be worked to give a straight, curved or pointed effect. When complete, the work is steam-pressed and the gathering threads are withdrawn.

Colour

Colour is an important aspect of smocking. Subtle effects can be obtained by using a self-colour like a blue thread on blue fabric; contrasting colours such as white on blue; or tones of one colour such as varying shades of blue on a blue background. For a dramatic effect, several contrasting colours such as purples and pinks on gold may be used.

The shape of smocking on a garment is an important consideration. The depth of smocking should always enhance and balance the garment.

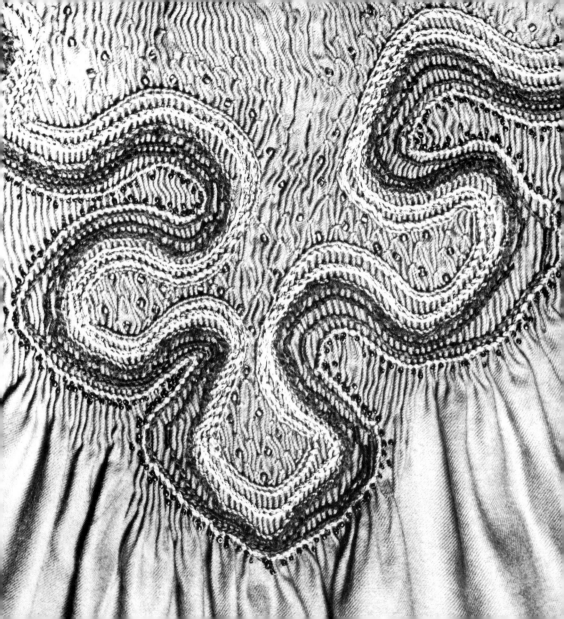

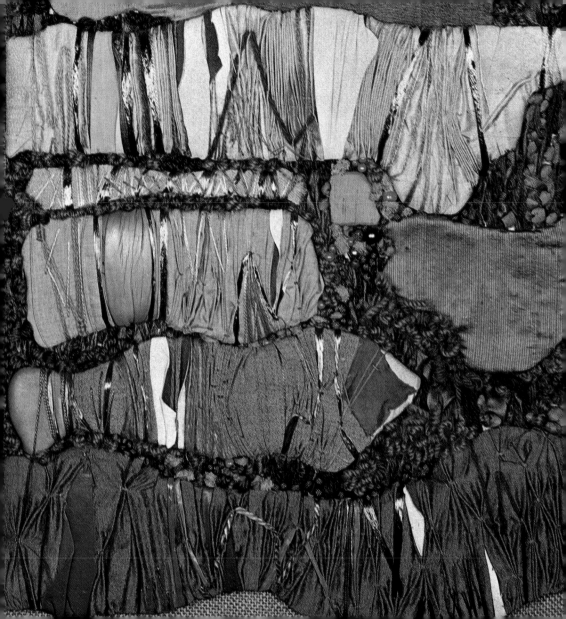

'Cotswold Wall' panel. Padded shapes incorporating textures such as smocking, ruching, pleating, tucking and stitchery (Diana Keay).

Materials

Fabric

Natural fibres such as wool, cotton, silk and linen, or man-made fibres and mixtures, either plain or printed can be used in any thickness, but bear in mind the draping quality for the finished article. For a delicate effect for a dress or night-gown for instance, georgettes, chiffons, sheers or voiles should be used. For a garment which has to give warmth and protection such as an outdoor dress or coat, it is better to use a stronger fabric such as linen, medium-weight wool or denim.

Once an understanding of working with these fabrics has been gained you can try the interesting effects achieved by working with more unusual fabrics such as velvets, needlecord, PVC, hessian, heavy furnishing fabrics, or even fine kid leather used in glove making.

Smocking hangs best with the drape of the gathers lengthwise with the grain of the fabric. It is best for a beginner to start on a plain-coloured fabric like poplin.

Thread for gathering

The thread for gathering needs to be strong enough to take the strain of gathering up. Sylko No. 40, which is used for ordinary machining, is recommended. Use a contrasting colour to that of the background fabric as the gathering threads will act as a guide when smocking.

Thread for embroidery

Embroidery threads such as Stranded Cotton, Perlé, or Coton à Broder are most often used. Stranded Cotton has the advantage that it can be separated for a thick and thin stitch effect. Perlé has a sheen which gives an interesting contrast. Several kinds of thread can be used on the same piece of work.

If a fabric is coarse, threads can be withdrawn from the background as in the cushion on page 19. Wools and lurex knitting yarns were used on the smock top on page 3.

For unusual fabrics experiment with more unusual threads.

Needles

These should suit the thread which has to fit through the eye of the needle easily. They should also be fine enough for the fabric. Crewel needles, which have long eyes, in varying sizes, are recommended.

Smocking dots

These are available as transfers and consist of strips of parallel rows of evenly-spaced dots which are ironed off on to the wrong side of the fabric as a guide for gathering, (Fig. 1).

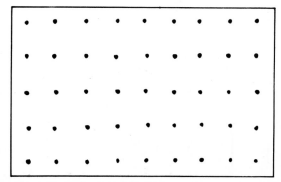

Fig. 1. Part of a smocking dot transfer

5

lat. Made of doubled nylon organza, and worked in wave stitch in stranded cotton (Diana Keay). Chiffon cuff. Man-made fabric. Worked in wave stitch with a fine needle for passing through the beads (Diana Keay).

Preparing the fabric

The width of material required depends on the type of fabric, the distance between the gathers, and upon the stitch and tension used. Some people work very tightly and others very loosely.

As a general rule it is best to allow three times the width of the finished smocking when calculating the width of the fabric. For a garment, the positioning of seams should be taken into account, and extra allowances made on the fabric width.

Before starting on a project, it is advisable to work a small sampler in the same material.

All preparation is done on the wrong side of the fabric which should first be pressed.

Applying smocking dot transfers
Cut off an edge from the transfer sheet and use for testing on a small piece of the fabric. The iron needs to be hot enough to transfer the wax dots quickly, but be very careful with man-made fabrics as excess heat can damage the material. When the iron is at the right setting, cut a strip of transfer dots to the required length and place it, wax side down on the wrong side of the fabric, using pins to keep it in position. Apply the iron, unpin, and quickly peel away the transfer. Sometimes the wax dots come through to the right side of the fabric but they should disappear after a few washes.

If you cannot obtain smocking dot transfers, there are a number of other ways for making dots on the fabric:
Ruler and pencil. Align the ruler with a thread of the fabric on the wrong side, and mark evenly-spaced dots with a hard pencil.

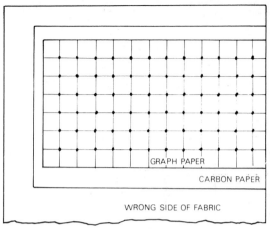

Fig. 2. Using a graph paper grid

Graph paper. Place a sheet of carbon paper face downwards on the wrong side of the fabric with the graph paper or hand-drawn grid pinned above it. Make a dot with a hard pencil at each intersection of the grid, (Fig. 2).

Template. Draw a grid on thin card and make holes with a stiletto or sharp thick needle at each intersection of the grid. Place the template over the wrong side of the fabric and insert a hard pencil through the holes.

Prick and pounce. Draw a grid on thick tracing paper and prick holes with a thick needle. Pin the paper to the wrong side of the fabric and transfer the dots by rubbing over with a small fabric bag containing powdered chalk for dark fabrics, or a mixture of powdered charcoal and chalk for light fabrics. Alternatively, the powder can be sprinkled on the holes and then rubbed in with a small roll of felt. Talcum powder may also be used. As the powder marks may not last very long, a fine artist's brush is used to apply watercolour or poster paint to the chalk dots before they disappear.

ild's dress. Fine wool. Smocked yoke and
ffs, the neck and sleeves finished off with
ench knots (Celia Batorijs).

Counting the threads. Where the warp and weft
reads are easily distinguishable, the fabric can
be prepared by counting the threads. Work on the
rong side of the fabric and pick up, for example,
vo threads and pass over six, according to the
pe of fabric and the size of the smocking
quired.

Tissue paper. For difficult fabrics, such as those
ith small detailed prints, it may be necessary
to tack either a smocking dot transfer or one
repared on tissue paper to the wrong side of the
bric. When the dots have been picked up through
e paper and fabric, the tacking holding the
ansfer in place is removed, and the paper is
ntly torn away. If this proves difficult, take a
arp needle and scratch the tissue paper deeply
etween the dots and the paper will lift off,
ig. 3).

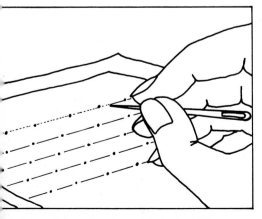

ig. 3. Scoring with a needle to remove tissue
aper

Transparent fabrics. Any of the already-
mentioned systems of dot transfers can be placed
under the fabric, wrong side uppermost. Pin and
then tack the fabric in position as flimsy fabric
will slip. Pick up the dots and then remove
tacking and pins.

Semi-transparent fabrics. Some fabrics can be
prepared as transparent fabrics if they are put up
against a flat window where the light will show
up the dots clearly. Place dots behind the fabric
with the wrong side uppermost. Pin and tack,
hold up to the light and mark with a hard pencil.

Preparing fabrics for straight smocking

When smocking is to be used on a garment, it is
done before the garment is made up. Seam
allowances should be taken into account.

For a piece of fabric, as in the case of a yoke or
a seam at the top of a sleeve, one extra row of
dots should be allowed at the top for gathering
and joining. This should be placed on the seam
line for a smooth join.

Straight smocking can be used as an inset in
a garment worked to the size of a lining of the
exact shape.

If the fabric frays, the edges should be whipped.

Measuring. Measure the fabric for smocking —
usually three times the finished width — and turn
the wrong side of the fabric upwards.

Transferring. Transfer dots of the required
length and depth on to the fabric, making sure
that the top line of dots runs along a thread of the
fabric. The lines of dots should be at right angles
to the grain or selvedge.

Gathering. Using Sylko or similar thread in a
contrasting colour from the fabric, cut a piece of
thread longer than the length of the row of dots.
It saves time to cut one long thread for each row
and keep them ready for use.

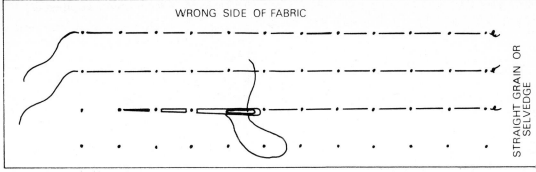

WRONG SIDE OF FABRIC

STRAIGHT GRAIN OR SELVEDGE

Fig. 4. Gathering from right to left

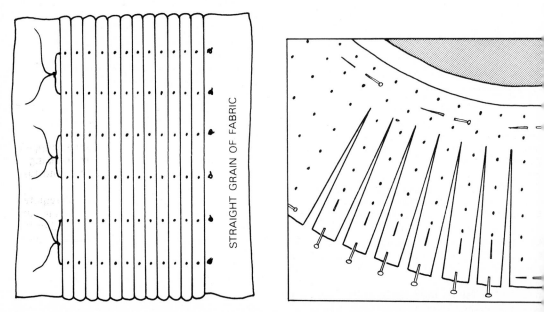

STRAIGHT GRAIN OF FABRIC

Fig. 5. Gathering threads pulled up and tied in pairs   *Fig. 6.* Preparing fabric for curved smocking

Starting on the right-hand side with a very strong and large knot, pick up each dot across the fabric, leaving the thread hanging at the end of each row.

Repeat until all rows are done, (Fig. 4).

Tying to the required width. Pull up all the gathering threads evenly to the required width for smocking. This will depend upon whether the smocking is done tightly or loosely, so adjust to fit, leaving enough room between the folds for a needle to be inserted. This is the most difficult part of smocking. Working a sample will help.

Tie off the threads securely in pairs, (Fig. 5). These pairs can be tied in pairs again for safety.

Turn the fabric over to the right side and the fabric is now ready for smocking.

Preparing fabric for curved smocking

This is mainly used on circular blouse-necks, such as a peasant-style blouse.

A strip of smocking dot transfer, or the tissue paper method, is prepared to fit the length and depth of the area of the garment to be smocked. Allow one extra row of dots at the top for binding and finishing.

If you are making a blouse, measure and cut out the fabric pieces for the blouse top, and join the seams. Pin the paper with dots, on the wrong side, along the top edge of the blouse. Cut between the paper dots from the bottom edge upwards to between the second and third row of dots. Spread the paper to fit the curved section and pin it in place, (Fig. 6). Transfer the dots to the fabric, marking in extra dots on the fabric along the curved area.

Continue as for straight smocking.

Preparing fabric for pointed smocking

This could be used on a skirt or any other garment where pointed smocking will enhance the appearance.

Any suitable method of transferring dots to the wrong side of the fabric can be used to the required length and depth. To shape the point, start at the bottom and leave four dots. Increase the width of the triangle by one dot each side until the point is the required length, (Fig. 7).

Continue as for straight smocking.

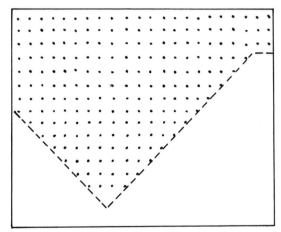

Fig. 7. Preparing fabric for pointed smocking

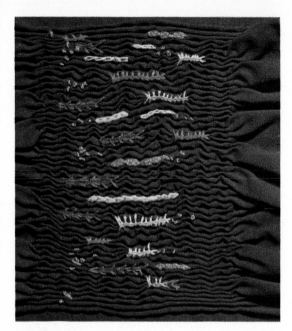

Navy-blue sample. A man-made fabric, cabled at the back, and decorated at the front with embroidery stitches (Diana Keay).

Stitches

Smocked stitches are worked on the right (as opposed to wrong) side of the fabric. Some stitches give a firm control, and others a more loose effect.

When smocking on a garment, allow for elasticity where the gathers are to fall, for example, a loose stitch should be worked at the bottom of a piece of smocking which is attached to a yoke.

Always work stitches at right angles to the folds by inserting the needle parallel to the gathering threads.

The first row of gathers should be left for joining on to another piece of fabric, for example, when a smocked piece is joined to a yoke. To keep the gathers in place the second row can be worked in stem stitch (see p. 15).

Work to as even a tension as you can through out a piece of work.

Starting and finishing
Start with a knot on the left-hand side by bringing the needle up on the left of the first fold.

To end, take the needle down beside the last fold and take it through to the back. Finish with two back stitches on the wrong side of a fold so that they will not be seen at the front of the work

If the thread is not long enough to finish a row take the needle down and finish off as above. Start again with a knot, making sure that the join is neat and unnoticeable, and as near as possible to the ending-off.

Two yellow samples. *(Left)* Stitches from top to bottom: Stem, mock chain, cable, double cable, basket, wave, close wave, spaced wave, trellis, diamond, two rows diamond, crossed diamond, vandyke, double vandyke. *(Right)* Stitches from top to bottom: Surface honeycomb, honeycomb, feather, bullion, herringbone (Diana Keay).

13

Mushroom soft sculpture. The cap and stem are made of tie-dyed velvet. The gills are gathered and smocked cotton (Jane Lemon).
Posy. Stylized flowerheads, padded and stiffened, made up from freely smocked circles of fabric (Jean Hearn).

14

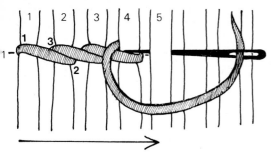

Stem stitch (Fig. 8)
Start on the left-hand side of the first fold at 1 and bring the needle up. With the thread below the needle, pick up the top (approx. 1mm) of the second fold, coming out at 3 and keeping the needle parallel to the line of gathering. Continue across the row with the thread below the needle and pick up each fold as described.

This is a tight stitch. It is used to set the folds at the top of a piece of work. It is sometimes called Rope or Outline Stitch.

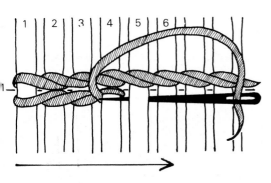

Mock chain stitch (Fig. 9)
Working from left to right, work one row of Stem stitch. Directly underneath work one row of Stem but with the thread above the needle, thus forming a chain effect.

This is a tight stitch.

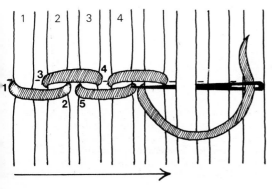

Cable stitch (Fig. 10)
Work from left to right. Bring the needle up on the left-hand side of the first fold at 1. With thread below the needle, pick up the top of the second fold, coming out at 3. With thread above the needle, pick up the top of the third fold, coming out at 5. Repeat across the row alternating the stitch as shown.

This is a tight stitch.

15

Cotton smock and belt (Dorothy Reglar).

Formal dress. Fine dark green wool smocked in contrasting colours, with added embroidery in chain stitch. A hand-made cord is used for the lacing (Dorothy Reglar).

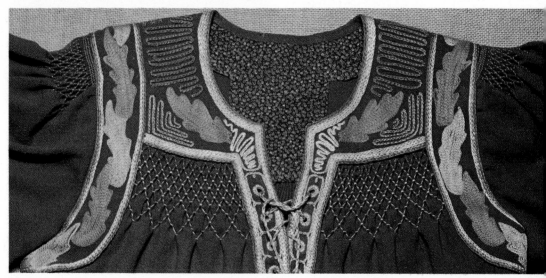

Child's dress and bonnet. Worked on pink checked cotton (Olive Camplin).

Party dress. Toning smocking on blue and white striped nylon (Olive Camplin).
Party dress. Blue smocking on white nylon (Olive Camplin).
Cotton bag. Striped cotton made into a bag, finished with a tassel (Rachel Newall).

17

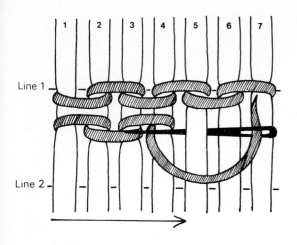

Double cable stitch (Fig. 11)
Work from left to right.

Work one row of Cable. Work second row of Cable immediately underneath to produce the cabled effect shown in the diagram.

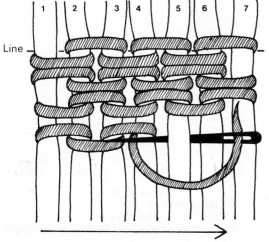

Basket stitch (Fig. 12)
Worked from left to right. Several rows of Double cable are worked. Shapes can be formed with Basket stitch.

This is a tight stitch.

Furnishing fabric cushion.
Furnishing fabric smocked
in honeycomb, using
threads withdrawn from
the fabric (Diana Keay).

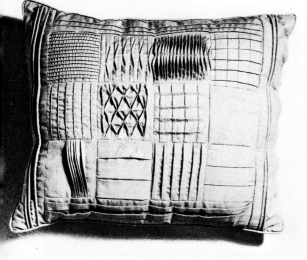

Poplin cushion. Samples of
tucking, one of which is
also smocked, sewn
together by patchwork
methods (Diana Keay).

19

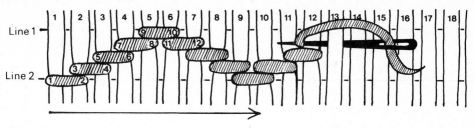

Wave stitch (Fig. 13)

Work from left to right. Make sure that the needle is parallel to the gathering threads. When ascending, pick up the top of each fold with the thread below the needle. When descending, pick up the top of each fold with the thread above the needle. A Cable stitch forms the top and bottom of the wave effect.

Start with the thread below the needle and work one Stem stitch, coming out at 3. Ascend with the thread below the needle, taking one Stem stitch on each fold until 9 is reached. With the thread above the needle, work one Cable stitch an then descend with the thread above the needle.

Wave stitch can be worked over any number o folds. It gives an elastic effect and is useful at th bottom of a piece of smocking attached to a yok

Close wave stitch. Work one row of Wave stitc Work another row immediately below and clos to it.

Spaced wave stitch. This is the same as Wav stitch but several rows are worked with eve spacing between each row.

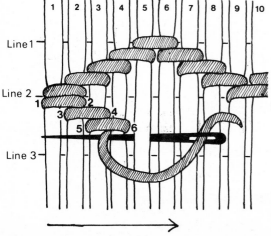

Trellis stitch (Fig. 14)

Work from left to right.

Work one row of Wave stitch. Starting o second line, and with thread above the needl work one Stem stitch from 1 to 2 coming out a 3, and descend as for Wave stitch until the thir line is reached. Continue with Wave stitch to th end of the row. Any number of rows of Wave ca be worked to form a trellis effect.

Coat Hanger. Made of cotton georgette, worke in Diamond stitch and decorated with lace flower (Diana Keay).

Pinafore dress and blouse. Man-made fabric. Traditional smocking in the colours of the pinafo have been worked on the blouse. The added embroidered motifs are taken from designs on old English smocks (Diana Keay).

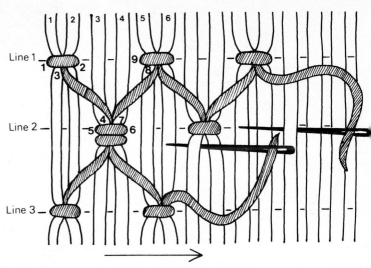

Diamond stitch (Fig. 15)

Work from left to right.

Bring the needle out on the left-hand side of the first fold at 1. With the thread above the needle, pick up the top of the second fold, coming out at 3. With thread above needle, pick up the top of the third fold, coming out at 5. With the thread below the needle, pick up the top of the fourth fold, coming out at 7. With the thread below the needle, pick up the top of the fifth fold, coming out at 9. Repeat across to the en of the row.

A second row can be worked starting on th third line as illustrated.

This is a very loose stitch.

Crossed diamond stitch. Work one row Diamond. Work another row over the Diamo row so that the stitch forms a cross by starting the second line.

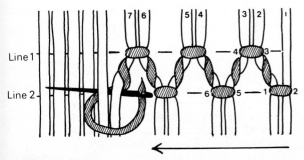

Vandyke stitch (Fig. 16)

Work from right to left. Do not make this stit too big. Bring the needle up on the left of th second fold from the right at 1. With the thre below the needle, insert the needle on the right the first fold, and pick up the tops of the fi and second fold together. With thread below th needle, pick up the tops of the second and thi folds together, coming out at 4. With thre above needle, pick up second and third fol

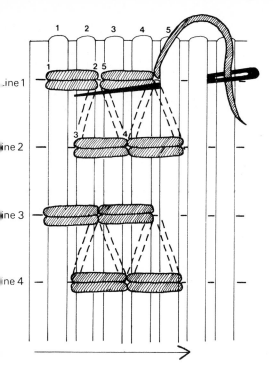

together again coming out at 4. With thread above needle, pick up the tops of third and fourth fold, coming out at 6. With thread under the needle, repeat, coming out at 6 again. Continue across the row.

This stitch is very elastic.

Honeycomb stitch (Fig. 17)
Work from left to right. Bring the needle up on the left of the first fold at 1. With thread above the needle, pick up the tops of the second and first fold, coming out at 1. Take needle across to 2, at the same time inserting it in a downward position in the channel of the second fold, so that the needle comes out at 3 on left of second fold. With thread under needle pick up the tops of third and second folds coming out at 3. Take needle across to 4, at the same time inserting it in an upward position, coming out at 5 on the left-hand side of third fold. Repeat across the row. The second row of honeycomb starts on the third line and goes down to the fourth line as shown in the diagram.

Honeycomb is very elastic and does not require so much material. Sometimes twice or two and a half times the finished width is sufficient.

Surface honeycomb stitch (Fig. 18)
Work from left to right.

Bring the needle out on the left of the first fold on Line 2. With thread below needle, pick up top of second fold, coming out at 3. With thread below needle, pick up top of second fold, coming out at 5. With thread above needle, pick up top of third fold coming out at 7. With thread above needle, pick up top of third fold, coming out at 9. Repeat across the row. For the second row, start on the second line immediately under 1.

This is a very elastic stitch and does not require so much material. Sometimes twice or two and a half times the finished width is sufficient.

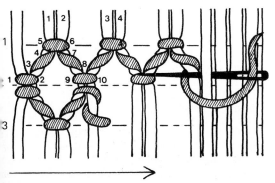

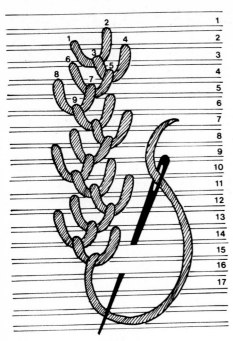

Fig. 20. Feather stitch

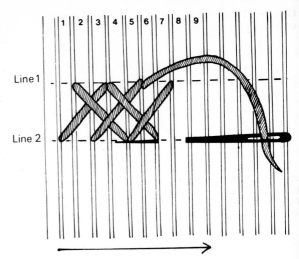

Fig. 19. Herringbone stitch

Embroidery stitches used for smocking

Embroidery stitches such as Feather (Fig. 20) and Herringbone (Fig. 19) are commonly used in smocking. As added trimming, Bullion, Lazy Daisy (for leaves) and Satin stitch spots can be used.

Feather stitch (Fig. 20)
Turn work so that this stitch is worked at right-angles to the folds as shown in the diagram.

Bullion stitch (Fig. 21)
Work this stitch over two or more folds as follows:
Insert the needle at A and bring through at B. Wrap thread around needle for the desired length, not too tightly. Hold the left thumb on the coils and swing the needle around to A and insert. Pull the thread through until the Bullion lies flat.
This stitch makes interesting rose buds.

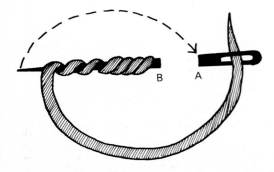

Fig. 21. Bullion stitch

24

ounterchange smocking. Worked in red thread
n black and white spotted fabric (Priscilla Taylor).

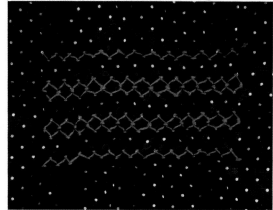

pron detail. Smocking worked on the squares
f lavender checked cotton (Olive Camplin).
ounterchange smocking. Worked on green and
hite checked fabric. (Diana Keay).

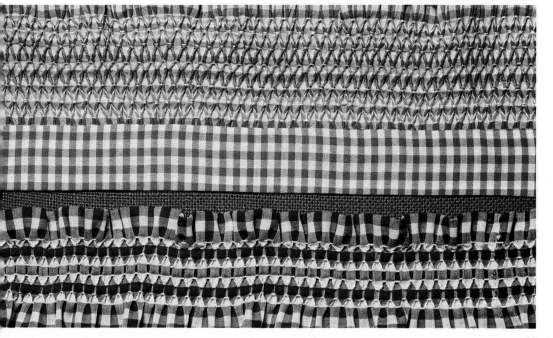

Finishing

Pressing
When a piece of smocking is completed it may
need to be steam-pressed on the wrong side with a
household steam iron. If a steam iron is not
available, place a folded towel or other thick
material on an ironing board or table. Lay the
finished piece of smocking on the towel, wrong
side uppermost, and cover with a damp cloth.
With a hot iron, pass lightly over the surface
without pressure, so that the smocking is not
flattened.

Removal of gathering threads
After steam-pressing, remove the gathering threads,
and the work is ready for making-up.
    If the sides of a piece of smocking need
neatening, in a child's dress, for example, a pin
tuck can be made on the wrong side as close as
possible to the ends of the smocked rows, (Fig. 22).

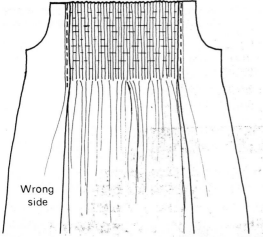

Fig. 22. Neatening sides of smocking with pin
tucks

Other types of smocking

Fabrics not requiring smocking dots
Some fabrics are so printed or woven that they d
not require elaborate dot preparation. The gatherin
thread can be worked straight on to the wron
side of squared (Fig. 23), striped (Fig. 24) o
spotted fabrics (Fig. 25), and then smocked. Chec
that the fabrics have been accurately printe
Woven pattern fabrics are reliable.

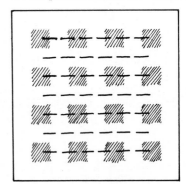

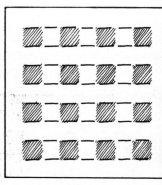

Fig. 23. Two methods for picking up squares on
the wrong side of fabrics such as gingham or tarta
Squares can also be used if the fabric is cut on th
bias.

26

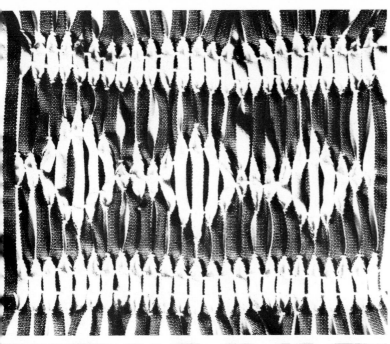

Counterchange smocking.
Worked on striped fabric
(Diana Keay).

Lattice pattern sample.
(Diana Keay).

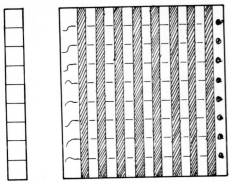

Fig. 24. Gauge for striped fabrics, and picking up stripes on the wrong side of the fabric after making a straight line along the top by creasing or pressing

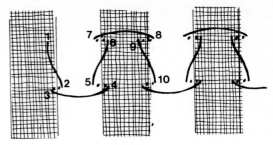

Fig. 26. Picking up stripes for counterchange smocking

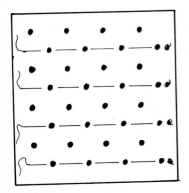

Fig. 25. Picking up spots on the wrong side of the fabric. Printed spots may not be accurate — woven dots are more reliable.

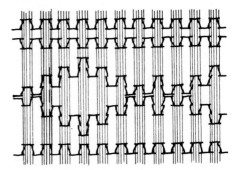

Fig. 27. Chart for working counterchange smocking on striped fabric

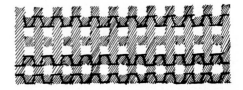

Fig. 28. Chart for working counterchange smocking on squared fabric

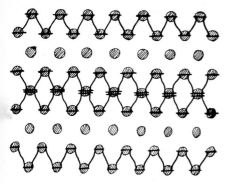

Fig. 29. Chart for working counterchange smocking on spotted fabric

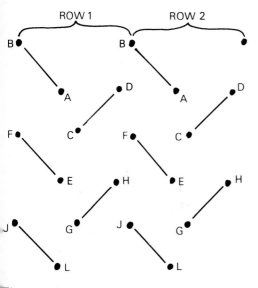

Fig. 30. Template for North-American lattice pattern

Counterchange smocking

This is a simple form of smocking on stripes, squares or spots, using surface honeycomb directly on to the right side of the fabric without any preparation. Choose a fabric with a suitable size of stripe, square or spot (Figs. 26, 27, 28, 29). A light or dark effect can be obtained, depending on which colour is picked up by the surface honeycomb embroidery. One colour of thread usually enhances this effect.

North-American smocking

This is a form of smocking which needs no foundation of gathering. By following a specified system of pleating, fabrics such as velvet and furnishing materials can be worked to produce interesting and rich effects. Strong linen thread, button thread or crochet cotton is used on the wrong side, but patterns can also be worked on the right side of the fabric.

Lattice pattern (Fig. 30). This is worked on the wrong side of the fabric. Velvets, corduroy and heavy furnishing fabrics, as well as satin and fine wools are suitable. Make a template in thin card using a stiletto or thick needle to make the holes, and transfer with dressmaker's chalk or light pencil to the wrong side of the fabric. Use strong thread for working.

Pick up dot A, (Fig. 31), and then make a small stitch over it. Pick up dot B. Return to dot A and pick it up again. Pull A and B tightly together. Pick up dot C. With thread above the needle, slip the needle under the thread between dots A/B and C and pull tightly to make a knot, keeping the fabric flat between A/B and C (Fig. 32). Pick up dot D. Then pick up dot C and pull together tightly and make a knot. Pick up dot E, and with the thread above the needle, slip needle under the thread between D and E and make a knot. Repeat down the work until the required depth has been worked. Work row 2 and repeat across the area.

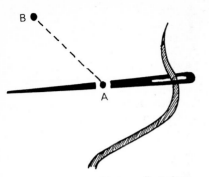

Fig. 31. Lattice pattern — first stage

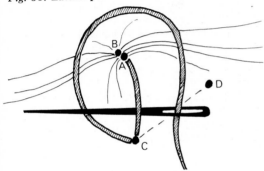

Fig. 32. Lattice pattern — second stage

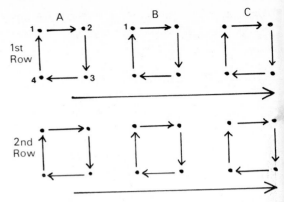

Fig. 33. Flower pattern

Flower pattern (Fig. 33). This is worked on the right side. Using a strong thread, start work at the left. Start at top left at 1A and take a small diagonal stitch, and likewise at 2, 3 and 4, slanting towards the centre. Pull the thread very tightly and take another small diagonal stitch to secure the dots. Take the needle to the wrong side, making sure that it does not catch any of the fabric, and bring it out at 1B and repeat. Work the necessary number across the row. Start the second row and repeat across the work. Work the required number of rows. The dots can be approximately 3cm apart.

Creative smocking

Once you have learned the basic stitches there are various ways of using the technique creatively.

Natural forms such as bark and mushrooms, rippled sand on beaches, freshly-ploughed fields, all suggest ideas for smocking.

Honeycomb stitching can be worked at random by taking several folds together to produce a creative result. Stem and Wave stitch can be made to travel in various directions by turning the work upside down.

Interesting effects can be obtained by cabling on the wrong side of a piece prepared for smocking, and then working embroidery stitches on the front. Couching can be done most effectively.

Beads make attractive additions to a smocked piece. Use a needle fine enough to pass through the beads and add them, one at a time, before each stitch is worked.

Beautiful effects can be achieved by tie-dyeing a smocked piece before the gathering threads are withdrawn.

Silk cushion. To make this circular cushion, a long strip of fabric was prepared with dots, and drawn up to make a circle. The centre was tightly worked on the wrong side in stem stitch, and the outer ring freely smocked in honeycomb (Diana Keay).

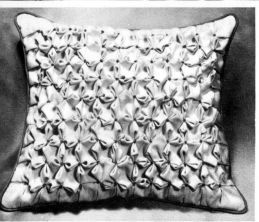

Flower pattern cushion. North American smocking, worked on synthetic linen and decorated with French knots (Diana Keay).

31

Acknowledgements

Edited by Kit Pyman

Text by Diana Keay

Diagrams by Jan Messent

Photographs by Search Press Studios

Text, illustrations, arrangement and typography copyright © Search Press Limited 1979.

First published in Great Britain in 1979 by
Search Press Limited, Wellwood, North Farm Road,
Tunbridge Wells, Kent TN2 3DR

Reprinted 1983

ISBN 0 85532 412 0

Made and printed in Italy by L.E.G.O. Vicenza

Frontispiece:
Boy's traditional smock. Made of fine linen, to the traditional pattern, incorporating feather stitch and buttonholed motifs, with hand-made buttons (Olive Camplin).

Front cover:
Silk tunic: Detail from smocked front panel on evening tunic (Celia Batorijs).

Back cover:
Tie-dyed sample. Rayon Dupion. The fabric was prepared and freely smocked and tie-dyed after smocking. Finally, the gathering threads were released (Diana Keay).